mediterranean *lifestyle*

mediterranean *lifestyle*

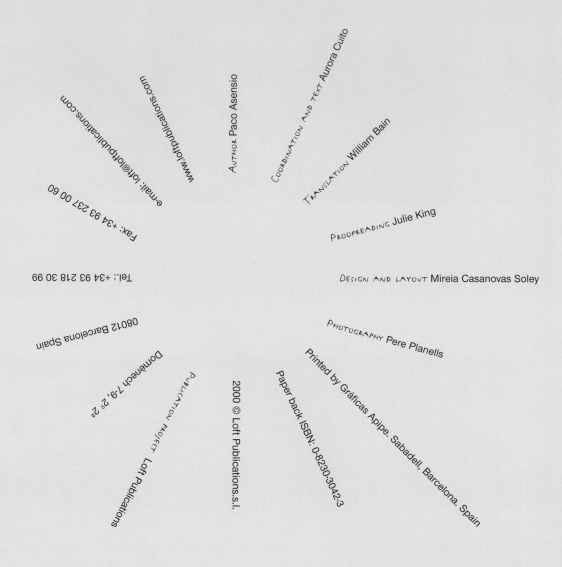

Author Paco Asensio

Coordination and text Aurora Cuito

Translation William Bain

Proofreading Julie King

Design and layout Mireia Casanovas Soley

Photography Pere Planells

Printed by Gráficas Apipe. Sabadell, Barcelona. Spain

Paper back ISBN: 0-8230-3042-3

2000 © Loft Publications.s.l.

Publication project Loft Publications

Domènech 7-9, 2° 2ª

08012 Barcelona Spain

Tel.: +34 93 218 30 99

Fax: +34 93 237 00 60

e-mail: loft@loftpublications.com

www.loftpublications.com

2000 © Loft Publications S.L. and HBI, an imprint of HarperCollins Publishers

First published in 2000 by LOFT and HBI, an imprint of HarperCollins Publishers 10 East 53rd St. New York, NY 10022-5299
Distributed in the U.S. and Canada by Watson-Guptill Publications 1515 Broadway New York, NY 10036 Telephone: (800) 451-1741 or (732) 363-4511 in NJ, AK, HI Fax: (732) 363-0338
Distributed throughout the rest of the world by HarperCollins International 10 East 53rd St. New York, NY 10022-5299 Fax: (212) 207-7654

POOLS TERRACES AND BALCONIES INTERIORS LIVING ROOMS DINING ROOMS BEDROOMS BATHROOMS KITCHENS GARDENS PATIOS FAÇADES ARCHITECTURE THE HOUSE WORK GASTRONOMY HANDICRAFTS LEISURE PEOPLE LIFESTYLE CITY MOUNTAIN COUNTRYSIDE SEA LANDSCAPE HISTORY

Introduction

The Mediterranean lifestyle is a subject broad enough to be daunting even to the bravest of souls. This book will approach the subject in four sections: a brief historical overview is followed by descriptions of where Mediterraneans live, how they work, and how they spend their free time.

The essence of the Mediterranean is one of contrasts between sea and mountain, sea and

desert, and sea and city. Its restricted geographic position, characteristic climate, and atmosphere of colors, scents and brilliance also distinguish this part of the earth from all others.

The book's approach is essentially pictorial, since the actions of the Mediterranean people are better explained through images, details, and moments of everyday life - folk festivals, architecture, decor, food, gastronomy, resources, the landscape, culture, and history - than through words.

The first section briefly outlines of Mediterranean history. Summarizing the history of this civilization in a few words is an impossible task, so we have chosen to mention the essential elements briefly, by way of reference only, to encourage readers to learn more about the area's fascinating past.

The book goes on to provide a tour of the various Mediterranean landscapes. This part highlights the sea, which offers magnificent panoramas: from vertiginous cliffs in Crete to heavenly Majorca beaches.

The fields, with their olive groves, vine-yards, and the like, continue to be a source of riches. The mountains, while not reaching the heights of the Alps, occupy most of the coastal area. The cities are where the most of the population live and are the commercial and cultural hubs. The third chapter is dedicated to different views of human activity, whether leisure or work. Despite the industrialization of the Mediterranean area, the most primitive work is presented: agriculture, fishing, and cattle raising. Of course, routine activities, such as shopping, which are part of the residents' daily lives, are not neglected.

Finally, the book presents the most private sanctum of the Mediterranean people: the house, including interiors and exteriors that reflect their users' personalities, longings, and whims. This architectural tour also includes the traditional means of defense against the inclement weather of this part of the world, offering carefully chosen details of facades, windows, doors, roofs, gardens, flooring, and materials. These details of color and light are, in the final analysis, what most clearly characterize the Mediterranean lifestyle.

HISTORY. THE MEDITERRANEAN WAS AND IS, DEFINITIVELY, THE CRADLE OF THE FIRST GREAT CIVILIZATIONS: EGYPT, GREECE, THE ROMAN EMPIRE AND THE CENTER OF THE WESTERN WORLD. ALL ARTISTIC AND PHILOSOPHICAL TRENDS HAVE ARISEN IN ONE LOCATION OR ANOTHER FROM THIS PROLIFIC SEA.

History

The social and cultural evolution of the Mediterranean has set the guidelines for contemporary Western society. The great civilizations (Babylon, Egypt, Greece, and Rome) were followed by the Middle Ages, which included two culturally splendid periods: the Romanesque and the Gothic. The first of these periods had the technical advances necessary to develop a heavy, austere architecture. During the Gothic period, building techniques were perfected to permit an increase in the height of the structures, resulting in such monumental works as the Church of Santa Maria del Mar in Barcelona or the Cathedral of Palma de Majorca. Artistic progress was directly related to a social revolution which was attempting to abolish feudalism. The changes produced in other parts of Europe, principally the French Revolution and the Industrial Revolution, established the bases of our society. In spite of the changes that occurred during the twentieth century and that have transformed Mediterranean society, it is impossible to understand the culture without first studying its rich historical past.

The photos in the center show constructions from different periods: a Neolithic dolmen, a medieval fortress, and two examples of Romanesque and Gothic works. The image on the right shows a bench in Barcelona by Antoni Gaudí, the architect par excellence of "modernisme".*

* "Modernisme" and "modernista" refer to the Catalan form of the international artistic movement known in England and France as Art Nouveau. The Catalan term is used here throughout the text as it refers to a very specific style.

LANDSCAPE. This chapter prese

Landscapes, not only maritime views, but a

provide an overall look at the territory su

A SAMPLE OF MAGNIFICENT MEDITERRANEAN
COUNTRY, CITY, AND MOUNTAIN SETTINGS THAT
NDING THE MEDITERRANEAN SEA.

sea

The Mediterranean was the first large sea to be discovered and named and the first to conquer the individuality of its setting. At the dawn of history, it emerged from the anonymity of the seas and oceans. Its name came to represent much more than all the other maritime extensions indistinctly forming the oceanic dominion of dark waters. Mythology, through the Hercules legend, already emphasized the idea that this sea and its land masses were the limits of the world known to Man. From the beginning, it was called a sea between lands, thus uniquely joining two opposing concepts: earth and water. It appears as the sea most accessible to men, the most human because it enjoys a more direct relation to the inhabitants of its shores. In spite of the fact that other seas have also played a similar role because of their small size—the Caribbean Sea, the Sea of Japan or the Sea of Celebes—only the Mediterranean has earned the privilege of being ours, the sea of mankind: Mare Nostrum. For centuries it was the only sea where a good part of humanity seemed to bunch together, to concentrate in this world center.

When we think of the *Mediterranean*, it is almost impossible not to associate it with the sun. Along with a *benign climate* that lets you enjoy the warmth of the solar rays throughout the year, these latitudes also have the advantage of offering some of the most splendid dawns and dusks imaginable. The reflections and other *plays of light* appearing on the sea are true delights for the senses. On the preceding page, bathers in *Rhodes*, Greece.

The Mediterranean offers *many advantages for sailing*. As there is scarcely any tide, entering and leaving ports is possible at any time of day. Waves break on the coast of *Formentera*.

The *coastal landscape* is characterized by rocky masses, natural *breakwaters*, rocks, *cliffs*... all these geological phenomena have provided sailing with a great many reference points. Thus, sailors have been able to easily find their bearings and have sometimes even done so without navigation charts. View of a fishing port in *Menorca*.

In spite of violent and dangerous winds in these regions, *rowing and sailing took possession of the Mediterranean* many centuries ago. At a time when land communications were insecure and had to overcome inexorable geographic barriers, a firm maritime system was established that would today be the equivalent of a *highway network.* Some islands—like *Naxos*—communicate with the exterior only by sea.

Landscape) *Sea* 19

In this region of light, sun and *temperate climate*, where the blue sea and the mountain are neighbors, where *magnificent places* as well as *artistic treasures* abound, where human history has left many traces of prestige, the Mediterranean appears as an ideal spot for repose, recreation and comfort. The tourist boom of the last few decades endangers the beauty of locations as authentic as *Saint Margaret's Island* in France.

The use of the sea for navigation was one of the fundamental needs of urban life. *Harbors brought together a population* that was more or less floating in search of new resources exploitable from the sea and new lands. Today, the citadel of *Bonifacio*, in Corsica, maintains itself thanks to *tourism*.

Cities were set up on naturally defensive sites, places difficult to attack. Sometimes they were established on separate islands, or else on peninsulas or on mountains where citadels could be built and which commanded the best views. This is the case in Genoa, Barcelona, Algers, Split... all of them cities built against mountains with scarcely an outlet to the interior.

Left: view of Saint-Tropez and, above, Grau du Roi, France.

From the sea the navigator can observe the earth from the point of view of *rough mountainous shapes*, often crumbling, sometimes in the form of fearful walls such as the *giddying cliffs* of Capri, the Costa Brava Crete.

There occurred a real battle between sea and mountain, the sea often cutting out *folds* that later brusquely disappeared into the depths, sometimes to reappear out at sea as islands. These images show the *citadel of Ibiza* and Cape Pertusato in Corsica.

Countryside

The study of life genres in the Mediterranean should begin with seaboard life; however, the fundamental base of human life on the periphery of this sea is more agricultural than maritime. Here, farming acquired an undoubted primacy and an exceptional density. The Mediterranean is the land of wheat, the country of wine and the region of the olive. This agricultural trinity was one of the essential causes for the arrival en masse to this zone of temptations: thoughts of satiating oneself on bread, wine and oil. But aside from being an agricultural paradise, the countryside surrounding the Mediterranean is wonderfully varied. While it reduces to a small territorial expanse, it boasts a wide variety of rural spots: arid, almost desertic zones, in the north of Algiers; rocky terrains in Libya; fertile swathes in the Valencian countryside; dry, inaccessible areas in Greece. But despite their diversity, all of these places have something in common: their incomparable beauty and an irresistible charm that has seduced their peoples and the tourists who have come to visit.

Large *sunflowers* color wide expanses of countryside in the *north of Italy*. Their oscillations and tone are intimately linked to the sun's location. During the day their orientation changes and turns to face the sun. The bright *yellow* darkens with the passage of *summer*, and harvesting is done when the sunflowers are completely toasted. The photograph above shows a field of lavender in *Vaission-la-Romaine* in Provence.

The prevalence of the vineyard populates the Mediterranean at least with *bushes* if not trees. Often the woodland itself was domesticated by converting it into a field or a subdued forest. A good example of this type of *agriculture* is the *corkoak* plantations in *Rousillon* or the *ilex* groves of *Turkey*. Due to *agricultural methods*, an important number of trees has been conserved in regions with sparsely populated woods.

"... IN THE SHADE OF THIS ANCIENT OLIVE TREE I CAN ONLY THINK ON THE LAND I LEFT BEHIND:
MY PARADISE, MY NOSTALGIA, MY LONGING..."

Homer
The Odyssey

In *Majorca* it was mainly *scrubs* that developed, with multiple and extensive root systems that seek the groundwater and thus compensate for the scarcity of rainfall. The scrubs adapt themselves to the *barrenness* and penetrate into solid rock. They are exceptional trees that demand little water and accept the severity of the summer sun because their *fruits* ripen only after the hot months, and their *harvesting* takes place in *fall or winter*.

The olive is the most typical Mediterranean tree. It is so closely associated with these regions that it is a characteristic symbol, and its distribution defines the border of the *autochthonous climate*, sometimes termed the olive climate. Thanks to this tree it was possible to exploit the dry, rocky slopes that make up the majority of Mediterranean lands. Different views of the countryside in the Greek *Peloponnese*.

In spite of the strong torrents of water the Mediterranean receives, its waters are extremely *salty*, which differentiates it from most of the other continental seas. Due to the constant and intense solarization, the waters undergo *high evaporation*. This reaction, along with the *strong winds* that blow in these latitudes, permits the abundant recovery of salt. These *saltworks* in *Ibiza*, flooded by seawater, collect large amounts of salt that is later used in many different ways.

The *lavender* in *Tuscany* is an aromatic perennial. It has a svelte gray stem and usually grows on rocky ground. The *essential oils* extracted from its closely packed flowers are used to make *lavender water*.

*T*he traditional *country house* characteristically has thick limed walls and small windows and doors. *Whitewashing* the fronts is better in isolated houses—like this one in *Cabo de Gata*—because if used in cities, reflection of the *sun's rays* would heat streets excessively.

*A*ll sedentary settlements were located near the *banks of a river or sea*. Easy access to water *conditioned* the choice of terrains to establish a town or city. Thus we find many instances of constructions over *water*. A fine sample of this is *Isle-sur-la-Sorgue*, in Provence, a small French town divided by the passage of a stream.

Mountain

The Mediterranean has become an *almost alpine sea*: in its basins and troughs a folding process has come about. The Alps, in some measure, arose from this sea and caused it to be intimately linked to Europe's largest mountain system. Right: a view of the surrounding landscape of *Tourette-sur-Loup*, in Provence.

On the shores of the Mediterranean, mountains dominate nearly three-quarters of the periphery. Almost everywhere massifs separate the sea from the continental zones of the interior and occupy the main part of the surrounding lands (a good demonstration of this rough geography is Greece, where 80% of the territory is above 500 meters). These peaks vary in height. The highest are brightly snow-covered, others belong to the domain of the shaded woods. In arid or windswept regions, many are carved down to live rock or eroded slopes. Green sierras, brown sierras, snow-covered sierras, and rocky sierras alternate on the borders of the sea with their distinctive silhouettes. They make up a very different landscape from the beaches with limitless horizons where the slope of the land is hardly perceptible under the burning sky. Here, in the Mediterranean, the mountain ranges appear everywhere; in reality, it is not a sea between the lands as its name indicates, but a domain enclosed by mountains.

In *Crete*, the mountain range in the center of the island is spectacular because of its luxuriant *vegetation*.

Detail of the *ochre-colored* quarries in *Roussillon*, France. The minerals extracted from these operations give the earth a reddish tone.

The high *winds* erode the rocky surfaces, causing *peculiar outlines* that resemble recognizable forms: human faces, animal profiles and other shapes that give flight to the imagination. This *erosion* is particularly great in *coastal zones*, like this impressive case in *Sardinia*.

City

The Mediterranean's first settlements were born around a temple and located in its environs. From these came the first traces of history after the long anonymity of prehistory. Cities were manifestations of a divinity and did not occupy themselves with any sort of material production, commercial exchange, or administrative matters. These cities were the first places that the most advanced elements of man's mental life were able to develop: arts, letters, sciences and, of course, religious life. Undoubtedly, this was one of the reasons why the city was a magnet that stimulated the Mediterranean people to become an ever more gregarious population. Slowly, the notion of city lost its religious support and utilitarian activities appeared, whether commercial, administrative or military. The use of the sea was another element that contributed to the formation of cities. People grouped together in ports in search of new resources to exploit in the sea.

If the public life of cities unfolds in *streets* and *squares,* it is also present in the importance given to sports, the theater, popular festivals and regattas. Above, a bar terrace in *Barcelona* and, right, a view of the *Cathedral of Palma de Mallorca.*

The mountains near the sea were favorite urban sites on which to construct *fortresses* or *acopoleis*. Maritime cities managed to isolate themselves on the land side and tried to live independently of the continent.

Barcelona —like other *port cities* such as Marseille, Venice, Athens or Algiers—has played a protagonist's role in the *commercial development* of the Mediterranean. During the *Middle Ages,* it became a city-state of powerful hegemony.

F ar away from the coast, many *settlements* sprang up near *rivers* or *lakes* in order to supply themselves with *water*. A magnificent example of this is the city of Gerona in Spain, on the banks of the Ter.

LIFESTYLE. THE MEDITERRANEAN'S CLIMATIC, GEOGRAPHICAL
AND CULTURAL DIVERSITIES ORIGINATE A FULL, RICH LIFESTYLE.
NOTABLE IS THE HOSPITALITY OF THE INHABITANTS,
WHICH GENERATES INTENSE SOCIAL
WHICH GENERATES INTENSE SOCIAL
RELATIONS AND A PLURALISM OF OPEN-AIR ACTIVITIES.

People

Owing to the climatic,

geographic and religious diversities that

are found in the Mediterranean basin, it is a zone

of mixtures and fusions. Its inhabitants are friendly and

hospitable: they like to socialize and exchange experiences,

traditions and merchandise. Besides, the climate lends itself to

open-air activities that promote mixing and communicating. The

streets and, above all, the squares of towns and cities become

improvised social centers that accommodate all sorts of events:

street markets, concerts, and popular fiestas. This social

effervescence confirms the Mediterranean peo-

ples' open nature and eagerness to

know other cultures. This is how

they become energetic travelers on

one hand and exceptional hosts on the other.

In these latitudes, and thanks to
a mild climate, a lot of free time is
dedicated to walking. Walks can
be interrupted by itinerant artists,
like these ones from *Aix-en-
Provence*.

Street markets like this one in Sineu, Majorca, are very common in coastal towns. Vendors set up each week in a different urban community and supply its inhabitants with goods which are not available in the town shops. Aside from food, they also offer other products such as kitchen utensils, crafts, clothing, plants, and flowers.

Some markets, like this one in *Valencia,* are set up weekly and are dedicated exclusively to buying and selling old books. They are meeting places for *intellectuals and collectors* seeking antique and rare pieces at the best price.

Markets are also the place to find *local products and handicrafts* such as *whole foods* (honey, cheeses, pastries...), handmade clothing, soaps and perfumes, jewelry and ceramics.

In the town of *Chaouen,* Morocco, the market has always been the place to exchange goods. The climate allows shops to set up in the *open air* in squares or on streets, covered by a tilt to ward off the sun's rays.

R ight: a view of the
Ramblas, Barcelona's choice
promenade.

*T*ypical dances in San José, Ibiza.

*T*he fiestas of *San Juan de Ciutadella,* in Menorca, are very popular. The arrival of summer is celebrated with equestrian spectacles in village squares. *Riders and horses* put on dazzling displays of their abililty and mastery by eluding spectators, who urge them to rear up and to jump.

C ities and towns celebrate their *patron saint festivals* with many different activities: concerts, processions, and dances. These photographs show some of the traditions celebrated in *Barcelona*.

Bullfighting festivals are both popular and controversial. While their detractors call them inhumane and cruel, aficionados say there is no more artistic and hair-raising spectacle. Incontestably, there is unusual enthusiasm in their attraction of devotees and tourists. *Las corridas* are held above all in the main area of *Spain* and the *south of France,* like this one in *Nîmes.*

Catholic countries celebrate *Twelfth Night* with its magic for all *children*. According to *tradition*, if kids have been good throughout the year, the Magi will bring them *presents*. On this page: the arrival of the Three Kings in *Almeria*.

Although invented in China, *fireworks* have become an extremely popular spectacle. In *Saint-Tropez* they signify the end of the summer celebrations.

Leisure

A temperate climate, the cordiality of its peoples, and the nearness to the sea make the Mediterranean basin the ideal place to relax, rest or spend a fantastic vacation. For one thing, the sea offers many recreational activities: sailing sports, diving, fishing, boating... and of course exquisite day-to-day pleasures like sunbathing on the beach or taking a plunge in crystal clear waters. Mountains near the sea bring the enjoyment of nature, pure air and temperate summer temperatures. Visitors can walk or practice adventure sports, enjoying an incomparable setting far from the burning summer sun. Finally, rural towns offer a wide range of social and cultural activities (concerts, popular fiestas, and street fairs). All of this has the added pleasure of a rich artistic and historical past that brings an enjoyment of the vestiges of past ages of glory.

Though the sea bottom is not highly populated by spectacular flora and fauna, the clearness and transparency of the waters attract a large number of curious bathers.

One of the most visited places is the Island of *Crete*. Its unending *beaches*, its high *mountains* and the authenticity of its spots of natural beauty make it a paradise for summer visitors.

In *sicily* the high number of *watersports* has endangered the balance of the ecosystem in some cases. Local authorities have declared certain zones *natural parks* in order to protect them from abuse.

A changing geography brings
about exciting landscapes: *sheer cliffs,*
and jagged rocks leading precariously
to the water, beaches of *volcanic sand...*
all setting for *idyllic vacations.*

The Andalusian character is an attraction for the tourists who visit the *south of Spain*. A bar in *Malaga.*

The portico of *Barcelona*'s Plaza Real has been invaded by bars whose terraces are protected from inclement weather.

One of the favorite ways to get acquainted with *Ibiza* is to meet in the *bars*. They have become choice social centers due to their locations and terraces.

Restaurant terrace in the *port of Haifa* in Israel.

Some old locales, like this modernist one in *Palma de Majorca,* have been *refurbished* without losing their original character. Design details make these commercial spaces unique and successful.

Handicrafts

Industrialization is very extensive throughout all the Mediterranean countries but this has not stopped people from continuing to create handmade products. Artisanship lives on thanks to firmly rooted traditions that are passed from generation to generation. The products made from raw materials are widely accepted in different cultures and are still used in daily life. The goods also interest tourists, which ensures their sale. Handcrafted products can be classified according to their original materials. Clay is the basis for all ceramic products, from kitchen utensils, to vases, tiles and other building elements. Woven plant fibers are made into baskets, bags, shoes, and even furniture when wicker is used. Finally, animal wools and cottons create an array of fabrics for garments and household items.

Potters' wheels are rotating tables, mechanical or electric, which turn concentrically to facilitate the shaping of clay. They are used basically to give form to vases or other ceramic elements of cylindrical or ovular shape. The clay is baked at high temperatures and later glazed.

These ceramic figures are typical of the *Balearic Islands*. They represent popular cultural characters and usually have two openings that turn them into whistles.

Ceramic tiles are widely used to finish surfaces that require a certain degree of impermeability. Thanks to their aesthetic value, they are also used as *decorative motifs* on façades, walls and benches.

Esparto, typical of the *Mediterranean coasts*, is a grass fiber that can be *woven*. It is used to make ropes, sandals, baskets and mats.

E*mbroidery* is a deeply
rooted tradition in villages,
where women get together to
decorate household items and
clothes with colored designs.

D etail of typical fabrics
from *French Provence*. The
Boutis combine
embroidery, textures,
relief and prints.

J *arapas* are typical of Los Alpujarras, a mountain zone in Andalusia. They are handmade and distinctive because of the lively colors in the alternation of plain and textured bands.

Gastronomy

Mediterranean cuisine is highly varied and extensive, since each region has its own typical dishes. However, the elements used to make them are repeated with variations and are based on local ingredients. The high amount of vegetable content is common; grains (like wheat and oats) stand out, as do green vegetables, legumes, and fruits (fresh or dried). Fish and shellfish are notable ingredients but meat (beef and lamb) and poultry (chicken and duck) are also very popular. There are other ingredients that characterize Mediterranean food: spices, for instance, mild in the north and piquant in the south, are a condiment that varies flavors. Manufactured products, like oil, cheese or wine are used alone or in combination.

Mediterranean *cuisine* enjoys a varied array of *tastes and textures*. It ranges from the simplest (like boiled vegetables) to the most sophisticated (like elaborate sauces, mix of fish and meat, or sweet and salty).

*B*esides the alimentary features of Mediterranean cuisine, one of its most relevant aspects is its plurality. There is a substantial number of *national cuisines* with their *regional variants* and they all influence each other mutually. Also, there are *sea cuisines* and *mountain cuisines*, and *workday and holiday cuisines*, not to mention *city and country festivals* or the *traditional* and *modern*.

*M*ilk products are *popular and abundant*. Although as a condiment *olive oil* is preferred to butter, *cheeses* and *yogurts* are present in every kitchen. Originally, because of the scarcity of pasturage, people used goat's milk. Today, cow's milk is more common.

V endor's stall displaying *goat cheeses* in a market in the south of *France*. They are seasoned with different spices that impart subtle taste differences.

Olives, green or black, are inedible when they are harvested. They can be processed to *extract oil* or *pickled* to remove their acidity and bitter taste. This preservation with aromatic herbs varies as does the flavor of the olive. On this page: an olive stand in *Saint-Tropez.*

Olives
2,90 Frs les 100 grs

S tall displaying a variety of *olives* at the Sunday market in *Nyons*.

B esides being one of the basics of traditional Mediterranean cuisine, olive oil was one of the *first products* that was marketed. *The Phoenicians* transported it in their galleys throughout the Mediterranean. *Olive oil* was used for *frying* or *stewing* and also raw as a *condiment* for salads.

The winemaking industry extends throughout the Mediterranean basin. Many of these wines enjoy a *designation of origin* that guarantees their quality. Outstanding, for instance, are Retsina from Greece, Penedès from Catalonia, Chianti from Italy, and Beaujolais from France. Right: a view of wine cellars in *Chateauneuf-du-Pape*, France.

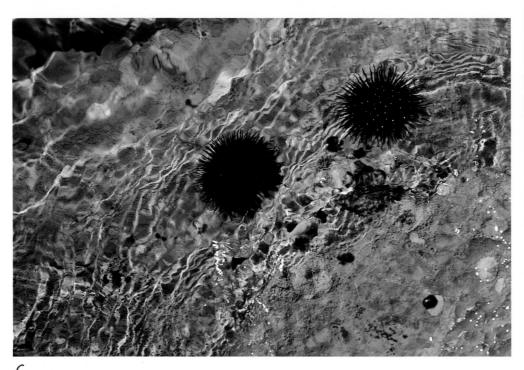

Seafood is one of the great
traditional riches of Mediterranean
cuisine: medieval recipes already
included a substantial number of
fish dishes. Among the most
appreciated fish species are
seabream, angler fish and sole;
popular shellfish include oysters,
mussels, shrimp, lobster and sea
urchins.

Detail of a crate of sardines at
the port of the small Greek island
Folegandros.

Work

This chapter attempts to provide a look at the

trades that originally developed in this area, without

analyzing its growing industrialization. Our visual tour

shows two vocational views related to the surroundings:

land and sea. While the Mediterranean permits abundant fish-

ing and commercial navigation, this is not what provides the prin-

cipal source of work. The population lives off the land more than the

water. Although fertile soil was scarce, it was possible to build up and

develop an especially prosperous agriculture by constructing well thought

out irrigation systems. The first products extracted from the fields were wheat,

wine and olives, which provided the essential food, drink, and ideal condiment.

Later, soil tillage was increased and perfected until it permitted self-supply and expor-

tation of the esteemed Mediterranean products to other parts of the world.

Taking advantage of its high *salt*
content, the Mediterranean has *saltworks*
located on different points of its coast. One of
the most productive is on *ibiza,* where
seawater is left in deposits to evaporate in
order to obtain the salt.

Contrary to popular belief, this sea is *relatively poor in aquatic fauna* because of the salinity and temperature of its waters. However, *fishing* has for centuries been a *main source of wealth.*

One of the most popular types of fishing in the Mediterranean is *light-fishing*. Fishermen set a *light in the boat's prow* and either use harpoons or cast nets over the illuminated *squid* and *sardines*. The scintillation of myriad moving stars on the quiet surface of the water is a surprising spectacle.

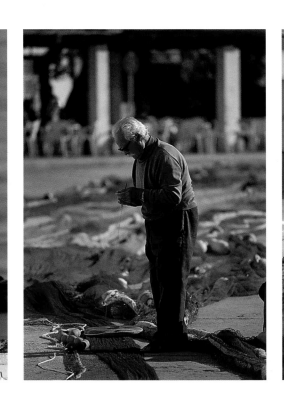

View of the fishing dock
and the marina of the
French town of *Cassis*.

In spite of the *modernization of ports* and the sophistication of fishing methods, there are still *small villages*, like this one near *Naples*, where fishing is done in the age-old way, using nets that must be untangled daily.

*B*uoys are attached to the edges of
the *nets* to keep them *afloat* and to
make it *easier to locate them* when the
fishermen return to inspect their catch
some hours later.

The Mediterranean *countryside* is covered
with *grapevines* that produce *very high-quality*
wines. The grape harvest, at the end of the
summer, is the busiest time of year since
there is only a limited time to pick the grapes
before they become overripe.

Picking and selling *linden blossom* in the *Bois-les-Baronnies*, France. Linden blossom has sedative properties and is drunk as an *infusion*.

Overleaf: view of a *Marseilles* market.

As the Mediterranean lands are unsuited to agriculture, they are extensively exploited for *livestock*. But pasturage is not abundant either, so *herds* tend to be *nomadic*. These images show two *farms* in *Corsica*.

A *shepherdess* keeps watch over her *herd* in the *Balearic islands*. She is dressed in clothing traditional to the area.

THE HOUSE IN THE MEDITERRA...

HOUSE, IT IS A QUESTION OF CONNECTING AND SATISFYING NEEDS FOR PRIVACY. EXTERIOR ELEMENTS LIKE TERRACES, BALCONIES, PATIOS AND GARDENS WERE CONCEIVED AS WORK PLACES BUT THEY PLAY AN IMPORTANT PART AS SOCIAL CENTERS AND CREATE A VARIETY OF ATMOSPHERES FOR THE WELL-BEING OF THEIR INHABITANTS.

Architecture

Popular Mediterranean architecture is the

result of a constructive process that consists in

creating buildings on a human scale with interesting

relationships that arise from a meaningful use of materials and

good placement. The Mediterranean basin, in general, lacks wood-

lands, but it has an abundance of stone, rocks, clay and sand. Masonry

has thus become the main form of building. When wood is available, it is used

for stairs, doors, frames and rafters. Additionally, contemporary architecture has been

influenced by modern society's requirements and many of the characteristics of cities have

undergone subtle changes. New stores have apeared on streets and avenues; the marketplace and

the beach promenade have filled up with bars; the whitewashed brick has given way to the concrete wall.

But although the impurities introduced by tourism or real estate speculation have left their mark on some areas,

the original structural network is so strong and the spaces so vital and dynamic that the genuine form survives.

Façades

Masonry, resistent and durable, is used for foundations and façades. The materials used are stone, dressed or in easily manageable pieces, or brick. The facings are commonly whitewashed stucco. The walls generally have a certain amount of thickness to increase their strength and their insulating capacities.

"THE BUILDER WHO LOOKS FOR A BEGINNING IS TAUGHT BY HIS FEELINGS FOR THE COMMUNITY AND BY INSPIRATIONS THAT COME FROM NATURE."

Louis I. Kahn
Prologue, *Popular Mediterranean Architecture*

106 Façades) The house

Whitewashed façades bestow
a special brightness to
Mediterranean houses and bring
out the contrast with other
objects placed on them, as is the
case with these potted plants.

Window shutters are made
of wood in traditional building.
They are *indispensable elements*
for darkening rooms and
preventing the sun's strongest
rays from overheating the
dwelling's interior.

For reasons that are almost
always aesthetic and fortuitous,
fronts are painted in *bright colors*.
In this Majorcan house, the
original liming is visible on the
frames of the lights and the lines
of the ironwork.

The Mediterranean house par excellence is characterized by the *whitewashing* of its façades. This chromatic technique meets *climatic demands* and compliments the serene, bright and radiant landscape. Details of popular houses in *Mikonos*, Greece.

*T*he *doors* are of a classic type that substitutes the rectangular form of the building's apertures by an *arch*. In former times, there was a strictly structural reason for this variation: *the arched lintel* diverts the *load* of the wall downward. This mechanism is now only a formal technique that sets off the entrance from the other lights. Left: an entrance in *Empordà*, Spain.

Patios

Inside the Mediterranean house, away from the ardors of the street, a special interior façade was created that could be opened for warmth to the dazzling rays of sunlight. The interior patio came into being as the Greco-Roman atrium, the Andalusian and Arabic patio. It was usually central, closed, often surrounded by arches and sometimes covered by a cloth or awning. It is adorned with shady plants that are arranged around a fountain that cools the area.

P atios that are used as summer
dining areas in *Malaga*.

The patio has many advantages: it wards off heat while providing *intimacy* that allows for a more secluded and solitary life. Patios are places that lend themselves to *open-air activities* without the inconveniences of public life. The previous page shows samples from *Gerona*, Spain; *Paros*, Greece; and *Provence*, France.

The term patio is also applied to exterior spaces with few plants that have a direct relationship with the house but are away from the street. They are often used as summer dining areas and are almost always covered by an awning or an osier screen.

Gardens

Ornamental gardens are the offspring of the market garden. They appeared when irrigation techniques developed to the point where accumulation or channeling of water made the care of plants and shrubs feasible and comfortable. Arabic civilization was the first to appreciate the shade of trees, the murmur of water from fountains, and the fragrance of flowers. Gardens are the result of this nature cult domesticated in the private domain. Once water scarcity is overcome, the Mediterranean climate is ideal for growing different local species that are well adapted to the inclemencies of the heat.

Of the *flowers* often seen in gardens, the *geranium* stands out. It requires very little water to thrive and still offers beautifully colored blossoms. The *cactus*, obviously, is another of the well-established plants, above all in *North Africa* and the *Eastern Mediterranean*.

120 Gardens) The house

The Mediterranean garden, unlike those in colder latitudes, is not usually entirely domesticated. Rigid geometric forms are avoided and more natural woodland extensions are chosen, without much outward sign of human intervention. Right: a private garden on Spain's Costa Brava.

Pines are the ideal coastal tree. Indifferent to an extreme climate and resistant of the *high whipping winds*, they bend and twist their branch structures. They need little soil in which to grow and are commonly found on very rugged *rocky ground*. Right: public gardens in *Cap Roig*, Spain.

The Mediterranean climate, *temperate* throughout most of the territory, is friendly to a *wide variety of flowers* that grow without much tending. Some species imported from other continents have adapted and *become naturalized* here.

Gardens by the sea need special attention due to the climatic features of temperature, humidity and wind in their worst extremes. Additionally the high degree of salinity of the sea water can affect certain species.

Pools

F ew structures better illustrate the culture of leisure and satis-

faction than the swimming pool. Certainly, its incorporation in the pri-

vate dwelling increases the quality of life, not only because of its intrinsic

advantages, but also because it implies the existence of a garden, a friend-

ly climate, and the possibility of living the open-air life. The pools on these

pages are the result of compositional considerations, from the startling

transformation of the immediate surroundings or from the careful integra-

tion between private and natural landscape.

Water is the center of this *Tunisian garden* that attempts to synthesize the *Arabic* and *Greco-Roman styles*. None of its elements is simply fortuitous but rather part of a precise symbolism. More than a place for physically bathing, the pool is meant to inspire the mind and the intellect..

The abundance of swimming pools in coastal zones shows how this element does not fulfill an absence but rather *constitutes an extension*, or a sophistication of a *beach culture*. Examples in *Ronda*, the *Costa Brava*, and *Capri*.

One of the *habitual resources* in pool design is *geometry*. The pure forms, lines and symmetries define the water surface and *organize the gardens,* following abstract and harmonious laws. Three instances from the *Costa de Levante,* Spain.

Pools

The location of pools must be carefully *studied*, taking into account the user's preferences and meeting a series of conditions such as the *orientation*, the *hours of sun*, the *presence of nearby trees*, and the views. A private pool in *Llafranc*.

One of the main qualities of this pool is its *orientation* and *integration into the Greek landscape*. The perimeter is a part of the bay that ends in a waterfall where the pool visually connects with the sea.

This swimming pool is built into an interior garden of an old city villa in *Brindisi,* Italy, with masonry walls and wide stone arches. A *succession of terraces* at different levels with various degrees of *isolation* and *different orientations* surrounds the entire pool.

Terraces and balconies

Terraces and balconies are a privilege, above all for those who live in the center of the city where the dominating landscape is asphalt. These exterior spaces allow contact with nature with the same measure of intimacy as that of the hearth. There is no pleasure like sharing summer meals and conversations in an attractive corner, whether lying on a lounge chair in the sun or protecting yourself from it in the shade of a porch, screen, or awning.

W hen the weather permits, long periods are spent on *terraces*. Normally, what is sought is an *integration* with the surrounding landscape.

On this terrace on the *Moroccan coast*, a *mythical style and layout* has been developed which emphasizes the relation to the exterior landscape has been developed. The elements shaping *the porches* are vegetation motifs, *wood* pillars and a *reeds* canopy. Some of the furnishings are also reed or *osier* pieces.

Terraces are used in many cases as *summer dining areas*. The tables are usually on porches or under tilts to protect them from the direct rays of the sun.

Traditional Mediterranean architecture is full of *open-air spaces* sheltered from the severe heat of the sun. *Modern structures* conserve the *rustic look* using *whitewashed stone walls, reed or osier awnings.*

There are terraces that are a *prolongation of the house* and, as such, use a decor more in keeping with interiors. *Framed artwork, lamps, tables* and *chairs* can be moved around.

interiors

Interior spaces reflect the personality of those who use them. This chapter, an excursion through the various rooms of the Mediterranean home, reveals the desires, caprices and longings of the people through their private domains. Most of the houses on these pages are rural constructions because they are traditional buildings that best conserve the original Mediterranean spirit. Each section deals with a different room - kitchen, dining room, living room, bedroom, and bathroom - and their specific role. Each family nucleus is organized according to tastes and needs and results in different distributions, some which prioritize and enlarge the common rooms and others that emphasize more private spaces..

Living rooms

The living rooms in these pages reflect the way Mediterranean people gather together to relax. These rooms are not the last word in style or the most recent trend in interior decoration, but they provide a glimpse of the personality of the people who use them: their habits, their caprices. The decoration of these places is the result of tradition, memory and experience. It develops by adapting itself to the passage of time and to new functional and aesthetic requirements. What these spaces have in common is the desire to achieve a warm and comfortable setting in which to relax.

Summer residences have magnificent terraces that are used as *open-air living rooms*. The hot climate makes *dawn and dusk* the ideal moments to enjoy them, when the senses are offered a true fiesta.

The decor of most Mediterranean houses includes *antiques*.
These pieces, *inherited* or *purchased* at flea markets and
specialized shops, instill a nostalgic feeling and are a reminder of
the zone's *rich artistic past*.

Many interiors have *white*
limed finishes that *illuminate*
the space. A house in *Baleares*
Islands.

Stone surfaces confer a certain *restraint* on the space while transforming it into a cooler area.

Many living rooms are laid out around a *fireplace*. Originally, it was an element that figured as the *center of the home,* for cooking and the only method of *heating* the dwelling. Today, with the appearance of other heating systems, fireplaces are associated with luxury: they bring warmth to a space but are functionally dispensable.

Above: various fireplaces in *Ibiza.*

Right: living room in *Empordà.*

*L*eft: a living room that keeps the *original setting* bestowed by the house. *Refurbishings* carried out on many traditional buildings tend to renovate the structural elements but conserve the house's feel and furnishings.

Liv

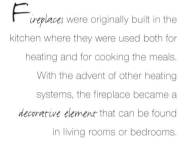

*F*ireplaces were originally built in the kitchen where they were used both for heating and for cooking the meals. With the advent of other heating systems, the fireplace became a *decorative element* that can be found in living rooms or bedrooms.

Mediterranean *living rooms*
connect directly with the exterior.
Sometimes by way of *oversize*
windows that facilitate enjoyment of
panoramas of surrounding
landscape, and at other times by
placement in the open air, sheltered
by tilts or porches.

Dining rooms

The importance of gastronomy in Mediterranean culture bestows a certain protagonism to the place where people dine. Meals, aside from being a nutritional priority, have become the most important social event. Family get-togethers, business gatherings, celebrations...all unite people around the dining room table. Thus, they are spaces carefully thought out for enjoying companionship and a meal in a warm and charming ambience.

The dining room is not a space that has strictly defined formal requisites. The only indispensable piece of furniture is a *table* and *chairs* or benches. The dining room of a house in *saignon*, France.

*S*ome of the examples shown display a *certain atmosphere of nobility*. Normally, they are found in *stately houses* that have preserved part of the original furniture.

At times the kitchen includes a table that is used for *breakfast* and for *family* meals. There is usually a *second dining room* in the house, used for *more formal meals.*

Good lighting for the table is advisable, whether natural or artificial. However, the proximity of a window could disturb those seated with their faces to the sun. The most effective solution is to install curtains that filter the light.

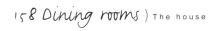

Dining rooms are usually fitted with *shelves* or *cupboards with glass doors* for storing *tableware* or crockery and other dining utensils. Normally, they are arranged as if it were a question of storing art objects.

M*editerranean dining rooms* connect directly with the exterior. Oversize windows often facilitate enjoyment of the surroundings landscape. Other times, dining rooms are placed directly in the open air and are sheltered by tilts or porches.

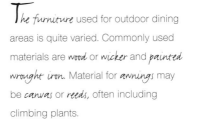

The furniture used for outdoor dining areas is quite varied. Commonly used materials are *wood* or *wicker* and *painted wrought iron*. Material for *awnings* may be *canvas* or *reeds*, often including climbing plants.

One of the privileges of living in the Mediterranean basin is being able to *dine in the open air*. The climate permits enjoyment of meals in *gardens, terraces* or on balconies. In summer, the tables are drawn into the shade to ward off inclement termperatures.

Bedrooms

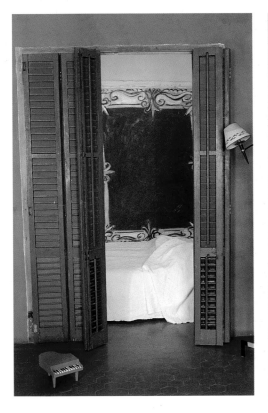

Bedrooms are the dwelling's reflection of its users' interior world. They are intimate spaces that make up the private domains of their inhabitants and, as such, are usually distributed according to their caprices and desires. In the Mediterranean house, sleeping quarters tend to occupy a privileged position that takes advantage of views of the sea or of direct contact with the outdoors, whether patio or garden. This chapter shows spaces designed to enjoy sweet dreams and magnificent awakenings by the sea.

Traditionally, beds include *headboards* which, aside from playing a functional role, confer character and style to the piece. There are two types: carved *wood* or forged *steel*.

The *master bedroom* generally has its own bathroom and leads directly to the exterior by way of *windows* or a *balcony* or even a door to the garden.

Given the proximity of the sea or of tideland, many beds incorporate *mosquito netting* to keep insects from interrupting peaceful sleep. Normally, they are hung from the ceiling, although at times they are part of the structure of the bed.

Harmonizing with the rest of the house, the bedrooms on these pages are *limed* to bring *light* into the space. Chromatic unification also includes bedding and other decorative elements.

The trousseau is the collection of household linen, above all the bedclothes, tablecloths and curtains. Tradition decrees that before the wedding, the bride's family gives her the trousseau, made up of sheets, rugs, towels...some made for the occasion and others passed on from generation to generation.

*B*edrooms are privileged
places often giving on to
the exterior.

*F*requently, *the bedroom* is
separated from the rest of the house
by *curtains*, above all if they
separate it from an office or a living
room. The space thus gains
amplitude and continuity during the
day, and privacy during the night.

Sleeping quarters, as *private domains*, usually have *decorative objects* of special interest, either for their *aesthetic value* or their *sentimental value*. This room shelters the dreams, memories and past of those who dwell in the house.

Tradition has it that the objects placed at the head of the bed influence our *psychic state*, altering, in specific ways, *our dreams*. Although nowadays this is only a superstition, the objects located above the bed still have an undeniable symbolic value.

Though it was not a common practice in the past, in the last few years there has been a tendency to create *open spaces*. This allows for *ambiguous atmospheres* where the domestic functions do not have set frontiers.

Bathrooms

While bathrooms are associated with clearly differentiated activities, they have a feature that distinguishes them from the other rooms: the use of water and the inevitable presence of specific fixtures and furnishings. The materials used are almost always different from those in the rest of the house. They must be water and humidity resistent. There is a tendency to consider baths as predominently functional spaces, to identify them with precise activities which condition the space. This chapter includes examples that explore different potentials using a variety of furnishings and materials.

Some refurbished *farmhouses* keep as much as possible of the *original structure* of the building. In addition, the materials used and the *baths and toilets* have been carefully chosen to harmonize with the rest of the house.

Mild temperatures throughout almost the entire year allow improvised *open-air showers*. They are water sources located on patios or in garden areas close to the house.

Manufacturers often produce
units that include all necessary
elements and anticipate their
installation and arrangement. In most
of the bathrooms on these pages,
prefabrication was avoided and the
spaces were exclusively designed
using unique materials and
furnishings.

This bath displays a certain scenographic ambience thanks to the effective and subtle distribution of its components, the well-chosen decorative motifs, and the placement and form of its mirror.

*A*bove all in traditional architecture, baths are observed to be small spaces that occupy relatively large rooms with a plurality of commodities. Direct access to the exterior by way of doors or windows provides views of surrounding landscapes while washing and dressing.

kitchens

Because of the functional role kitchens play, we have a predefined and exclusive image of them. This chapter presents spaces that combine a large number of materials and furnishings that encourage other activities besides gastronomy. Thus, kitchens become rooms where other tasks can be carried out: meeting with those who share the house, studying, watching television, working.... The selection focuses on rural kitchens, since they maintain the traditional Mediterranean style.

A kitchen is a predominantly functional space. It should include different storage elements, for tableware, crockery and other items, and food.

In some of the examples here, the shelves and cabinets are open or have glass doors. In this manner, porcelain bowls, spice boxes or ceramic ware make up part of the space's decor.

Left: a stand displaying *spices*. The immense role played by aromatic herbs in *Mediterranean cooking* should not be overlooked. Some are local, but a great variety come from other regions.

In past times, food was preserved in glass or clay containers along with *natural substances* that kept them from deteriorating. These natural preservatives varied according to the foodstuffs they protected.

*T*wo *zones* are often distinguishable in kitchens, one for *preparing meals* and another for the table where *family meals* are served. This incorporated dining area is often used with greater frequency than the main dining room, above all for the sake of convenience.

The objects arranged on shelves accumulate dust and *curtains* are sometimes used to protect kitchenware and to provide the kitchen with a *thematic image*.

STYLISM

Elena Calderón
p.100, 101, 103, 112 top, 115, 116 bottom center., 117, 125, 131, 134, 135, 139, 140, 146 bottom left center, 148, 151, 152, 153, 154 top, 155, 156 bottom, 157, 158, 159, 160, 162, 166 bottom, 167, 168, 169, 171, 173, 174 right, 178 bottom, 179, 182, 183, 186 bottom, 187, 188 top, 189, 190, 191 left

Àngels G. Giró
p.66 bottom, 106, 107, 112 bottom 116 top left center, 126, 127, 138 bottom, 142, 143, 144 left, 145, 150 top left bottom, 156 top, 164 left., 165, 166 top center, 176 right, 178 top, 181, 185, 187 left

The authors wish to convey their very special thanks to the following people, without whose inestimable collaboration this book would not have been possible:

Esther Arpa, Neus Artiga & Xavi Roca, Eduardo Arruaga & Francisco Sabidó, Sergi Bastidas, Michel Biehn, Rolf Blackstad, M.& Mme. Blieck, Stephan & Frances Burgeois, Rafael Calparsoro, Mary Cantarell, Norman Cinamond, Cecilia Conde, Grillo Demo, Karen & John Dyson, Antonio Facchini, Nuria Ferrer & G.C.A. Arquitectes Associats, Guillem Frontera, Babette Gabarró, Angels G. Giró, Caty Heunoumont & Renaud Bossert, Heinz & Ute Mack, Chicho Londaiz, Federico Manzano, Jörg Marquard, Sra. Mas, Marta Medina, Giovanni Melillo, Luis R. Mori, Angel Nieto, Toni Obrador, Pascua Ortega, Christian & Tomasa & Ion Pananides, Gabriel Paricio, Françoise Pialoux, Antonio Prat, Kamila Regent & Pierre Jaccaud & Nora, Teresa Reyes, Merche Romeu, Myriam Sagastizabal, Estrella Salietti, Mr. & Mrs. Scott, Leandro Silva, Ricardo Urgell & Maria Calderon & Iria, Juan Ramón Vidal, Joana Villalonga, Nona Von Haeften & Wolf Siegfried Wagner, Claire Webster

And also to: Yves, Alain,Vicente, Angel, Virginia, Antonio, Luis, Toni, Isabel, Alain, Aicha, Sara, Guillem, Paquita, Xesca, Anna, Guedea, Luis, Olivia, Manel & Monica, Quico & Rosa, Margaret, Chon, Conxita, Teresa, Katharina, Lisa, Hellas, Susana, Yolanda, Antonis.